THE Baby Boomer's SONGBOOK

65 Hit Songs!

ISBN 0-634-00547-2

HAL•LEONARD® CORPORATION

7777 W. BLUEMOUND RD. P.O. BOX 13819 MILWAUKEE, WI 53213

Visit Hal Leonard Online at
www.halleonard.com

Contents

Contents by Category

All You Need Is Love

Words and Music by JOHN LENNON
and PAUL McCARTNEY

CALIFORNIA DREAMIN'

Words and Music by JOHN PHILLIPS
and MICHELLE PHILLIPS

Medium Rock beat

All the leaves are brown, And the sky is grey.

I've been for a walk on a win-ter's day.

I'd be safe and warm, if I was in L. A.
If I did-n't tell her I could leave to-day.

MCA Music Publishing

BABY LOVE

Words and Music by BRIAN HOLLAND,
EDWARD HOLLAND and LAMONT DOZIER

CHERISH

Words and Music by
TERRY KIRKMAN

Cher-ish is the word I use to de-scribe _____
Per-ish is the word that more than ap-plies _____

all the feel-ing that I have hid-ing here for you in-side. _____
to the hope in my heart each time I re-a-lize _____

You don't know how man-y times I've wished that I had
that I am not gon-na be the one to share your

CRYING

Words and Music by ROY ORBISON
and JOE MELSON

I Heard It Through the Grapevine

Words and Music by NORMAN J. WHITFIELD
and BARRETT STRONG

Moderately
N.C.

Mm. _____ I bet you're won-derin' how I knew
___ ain't sup-posed to cry,
___ of what you see,

'bout your plans ___ to make me blue, ___ with some oth-er guy ___
but these tears ___ I can't hold in - side. ___ Los - in' you ___
son, and none ___ of what you hear. ___ But I can't help ___

I WANT TO HOLD YOUR HAND

Words and Music by JOHN LENNON
and PAUL McCARTNEY

MY BOYFRIEND'S BACK

Words and Music by ROBERT FELDMAN,
GERALD GOLDSTEIN and RICHARD GOTTEHRER

MY CHERIE AMOUR

Words and Music by STEVIE WONDER,
SYLVIA MOY and HENRY COSBY

MY GIRL

Words and Music by WILLIAM "SMOKEY" ROBINSON
and RONALD WHITE

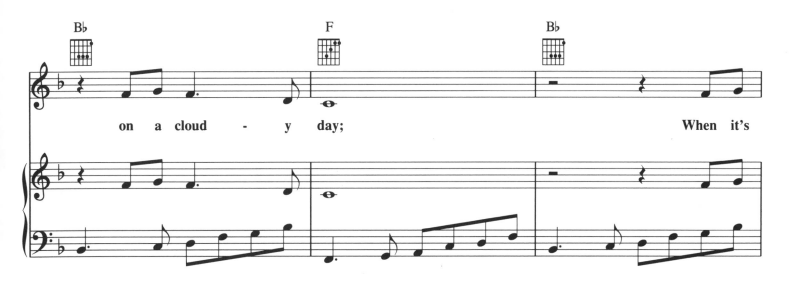

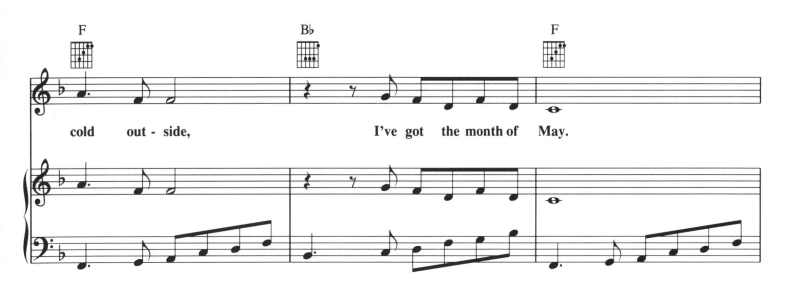

SOMETHING

Words and Music by
GEORGE HARRISON

Some- thing in___ the way___ she moves,___
Some- where in___ her smile___ she knows,___
Some- thing in___ the way___ she knows,___

at- tracts___ me like___ no oth- er lov- er.
that I___ don't need___ no oth- er lov- er.
and all___ I have___ to do is think___ of her.

Some- thing in___ the way___ she woos___ me.
Some- thing in her style___ that shows___ me.
Some- thing in___ the things___ she shows___ me.

I don't want to leave___ her now,   you

STAND BY ME
featured in the Motion Picture STAND BY ME

Words and Music by BEN E. KING,
JERRY LEIBER and MIKE STOLLER

Slowly

When the night_____ has come and the land is dark And the moon_____ is the on-ly_____ light we'll see, No, I won't be a-fraid, no_____ I_____

SUNSHINE SUPERMAN

Words and Music by
DONOVAN LEITCH

♩=135

1. Sun-shine came soft-ly through my win-dow to-day,—
(Verses 2, 3, 4 & 5 see block lyric)

could have tripped out ea-sy but I've changed my ways,—

⊕ *Coda*

I'll pick up your hand— and slow- ly   blow your lit- tle mind.—

Verse 2:
Superman and Green Lantern ain't got nothing on me
I can make like a turtle and dive for pearls in the sea
You can just sit there thinking on your velvet throne
I've followed the rainbow so you can have all your own.

'Cause I've made my mind up you're going to be mine.
I'll tell you right now
Any trick in the book now baby that I can find.

Verse 3:
Everybody's hustling just to have a little scene
When I said we'd be cool I think that you know what I mean.
We stood on a beach at sunset, do you remember when?
I know a beach where baby, it never ends.

When you've made your mind up forever to be mine.
Mmm.... *(to 3° bar)*

Verse 4:
Instrumental

Verse 5:
Superman and Green Lantern ain't got nothing on me
I can make like a turtle and dive for pearls in the sea
You can just sit there thinking on your velvet throne
I've followed the rainbow so you can have all your own.

When you've made your mind up forever to be mine.
Mmm.... *(to 5° bar)*

WEDDING BELL BLUES

Words and Music by
LAURA NYRO

WILL YOU LOVE ME TOMORROW

(Will You Still Love Me Tomorrow)

Words and Music by GERRY GOFFIN
and CAROLE KING

SURFIN' U.S.A.

Written by CHUCK BERRY
and BRIAN WILSON

BEST OF MY LOVE

Words and Music by JOHN DAVID SOUTHER,
DON HENLEY and GLENN FREY

AMERICAN PIE

Words and Music by
DON McLEAN

Lyrics:

A long, long time a-go I can still re-mem-ber how that

mu-sic used to make me smile. And

I knew if I had my chance that I could make those peo-ple dance and

may-be they'd be hap-py for a while.

MCA Music Publishing

Additional Lyrics

2. Now for ten years we've been on our own,
And moss grows fat on a rollin' stone
But that's not how it used to be
When the jester sang for the king and queen
In a coat he borrowed from James Dean
And a voice that came from you and me
Oh and while the king was looking down,
The jester stole his thorny crown
The courtroom was adjourned,
No verdict was returned
And while Lenin read a book on Marx
The quartet practiced in the park
And we sang dirges in the dark
The day the music died
We were singin'... bye-bye... etc.

3. Helter-skelter in the summer swelter
The birds flew off with a fallout shelter
Eight miles high and fallin' fast,
it landed foul on the grass
The players tried for a forward pass,
With the jester on the sidelines in a cast
Now the half-time air was sweet perfume
While the sergeants played a marching tune
We all got up to dance
But we never got the chance
'Cause the players tried to take the field,
The marching band refused to yield
Do you recall what was revealed
The day the music died
We started singin'... bye-bye... etc.

4. And there we were all in one place,
A generation lost in space
With no time left to start again
So come on, Jack be nimble, Jack be quick,
Jack Flash sat on a candlestick
'Cause fire is the devil's only friend
And as I watched him on the stage
My hands were clenched in fists of rage
No angel born in hell
Could break that Satan's spell
And as the flames climbed high into the night
To light the sacrificial rite
I saw Satan laughing with delight
The day the music died
He was singin'... bye-bye... etc.

AT SEVENTEEN

Words and Music by
JANIS IAN

Could It Be Magic

Words and Music by ADRIENNE ANDERSON
and BARRY MANILOW

84

DON'T LET THE SUN GO DOWN ON ME

featured in the Motion Picture LOST BOYS

Words and Music by ELTON JOHN
and BERNIE TAUPIN

Slow beat

I can't light no more of your dark - ness

All my pic - tures seem to fade to black and white

I'm grow-ing tired and time stands still be-fore

THE FIRST TIME EVER I SAW YOUR FACE

Words and Music by
EWAN MacCOLL

I WILL SURVIVE

Words and Music by DINO FEKARIS
and FREDDIE PERREN

IF

Words and Music by
DAVID GATES

IF YOU LEAVE ME NOW

Words and Music by
PETER CETERA

IMAGINE

Words and Music by
JOHN LENNON

Im-ag-ine there's no hea-ven.

It's eas-y if you try.

No hell below us,

LOVE WILL KEEP US TOGETHER

Words and Music by NEIL SEDAKA
and HOWARD GREENFIELD

Moderately

Love, love will keep us to-geth - er;
You, you be - long to me now;
will be there to share for-ev - er;

think of me, babe, when-ev - er some sweet-talk - in' guy comes a-long,
ain't gon - na set you free now. When those guys start hang-in' a-round,
love will keep us to-geth - er. Said it be-fore and I'll say it a-gain, while

sing-in' his song. Don't mess a - round; you got-ta be strong. Just
talk-in' me down, hear with your heart and you won't hear a sound. Just
oth - ers pre-tend, I need you now and I'll need you then.

Sometimes When We Touch

Words by DAN HILL
Music by BARRY MANN

Slowly, in 2

Lyrics:

ask me if___ I love___ you,___ and I choke on my___ re-ply.___
mance and all___ its strat- e - gy leaves me bat- tling with___ my pride.___
times I un- der-stand___ you,___ and I know how hard___ you've tried.___

RIKKI DON'T LOSE THAT NUMBER

Words and Music by WALTER BECKER
and DONALD FAGEN

SIR DUKE

Words and Music by
STEVIE WONDER

Mu- sic is a world with- in it- self _____ with a
Mu- sic knows it is and al- ways will _____ be one of

lan- guage we all un- der- stand, _____
the things that life just won't quit. _____

TONIGHT'S THE NIGHT
(Gonna Be Alright)

Words and Music by
ROD STEWART

Stay a-way __ from my win-dow; stay a-way __ from my back door too. __ Dis-con-nect the tel-e-phone __ line; __ re-lax, ba-by, and draw that blind. __

YOU'RE SO VAIN

Words and Music by
CARLY SIMON

YOU'VE GOT A FRIEND

Words and Music by
CAROLE KING

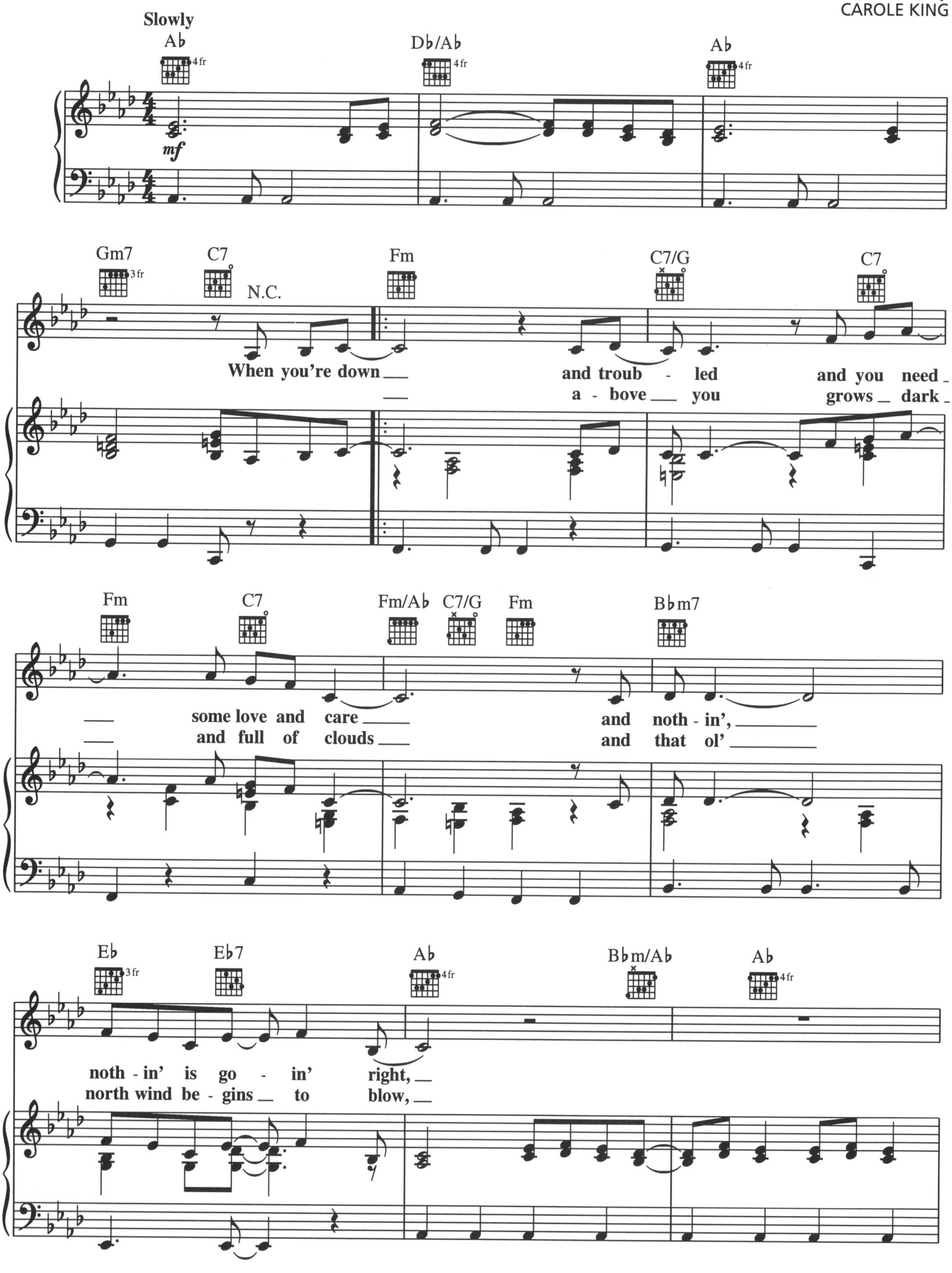

BANDSTAND BOOGIE
from the Television Series AMERICAN BANDSTAND

Words by BARRY MANILOW and BRUCE SUSSMAN
Music by CHARLES ALBERTINE

Fast Swing

We're go - in' hop - pin', (Hop!) we're go - in' hop - pin' to - day, where things are
swing - in', (Swing!) we're gon - na swing in the crowd, and we'll be

pop - pin' (Pop!) the Phil - a - del - phi - a way; we're gon - na drop in (Drop!) on all the
cling - in' (Cling!) and float - in' high on a cloud, the phones are ring - in' (Ring!) my mom and

THE ADDAMS FAMILY THEME

Theme from the TV Show and Movie

Music and Lyrics by
VIC MIZZY

They're creep-y and they're kook-y, mys-te-ri-ous and spook-y, they're al-to-geth-er ook-y, the Add-ams Fam-i-ly. Their house is a mu-se-um, where

BALLAD OF JED CLAMPETT

from the Television Series THE BEVERLY HILLBILLIES

Words and Music by
PAUL HENNING

Come and lis - ten to my sto - ry 'bout a man named Jed,
first thing you know old Jed's a mil - lion-aire,
Jed bought a man-sion, law - dy, it was swank,
now it's time to say good-bye to Jed and all his kin.

poor moun - tain-eer, bare - ly kept his fam - 'ly fed. And
kin - folk said, "Jed, move a - way from there." Said,
next door neigh - bor was the pres - 'dent of the bank. Lot - sa
They would like to thank you folks for kind - ly drop - pin' in. You're

THEME FROM "BEWITCHED"
from the Television Series

Words and Music by JACK KELLER
and HOWARD GREENFIELD

Be - witched,__ be - witched,__ you've got me in your spell.__

Be - witched,__ be - witched,__ you

know your craft so well.__ Be - fore I knew__ what

THE BRADY BUNCH

Theme from the Paramount Television Series THE BRADY BUNCH

Words and Music by SHERWOOD SCHWARTZ
and FRANK DEVOL

COURTSHIP OF EDDIE'S FATHER

from the Television Series

Words and Music by
HARRY NILSSON

JEANNIE
Theme from I DREAM OF JEANNIE

By HUGH MONTENEGRO
and BUDDY KAYE

COME ON GET HAPPY

Theme from THE PARTRIDGE FAMILY

Words and Music by WES FARRELL
and DANNY JANSSEN

Hel - lo world _ hear the song _ that we're sing - in';

come on get hap - py. _

A whole lot of lov - in' is what _ we'll be bring - in', we'll make you hap -

THEME FROM "THE MONKEES"
(Hey, Hey We're The Monkees)
from the Television Series THE MONKEES

Words and Music by TOMMY BOYCE
and BOBBY HART

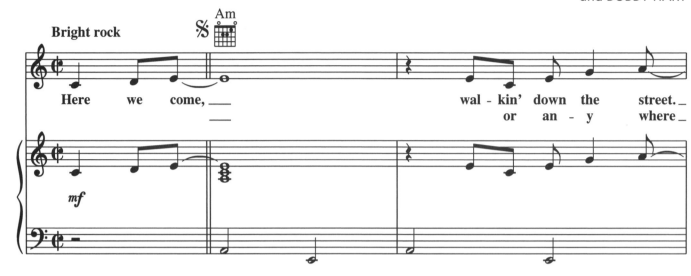

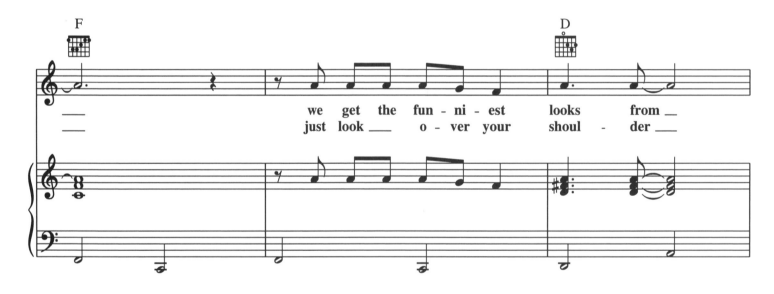

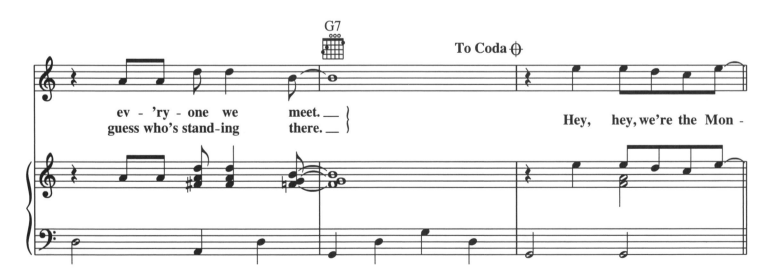

Theme from "Star Trek®"

from the Paramount Television Series STAR TREK

Words by GENE RODDENBERRY
Music by ALEXANDER COURAGE

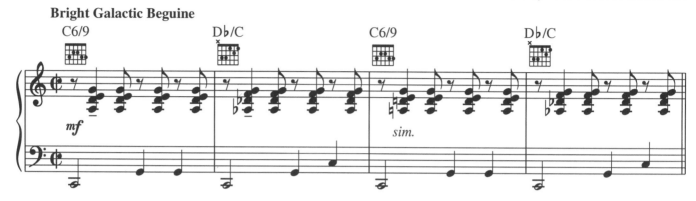

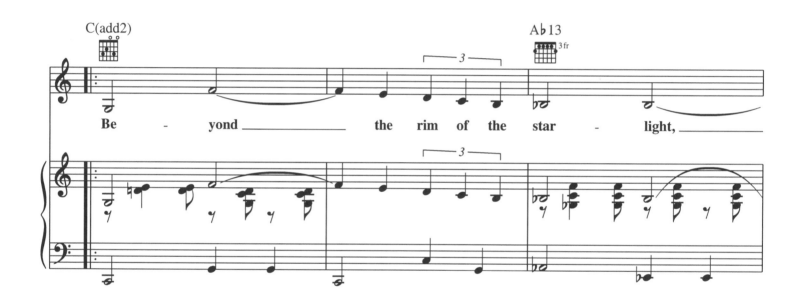

Be - yond _____ the rim of the star - light, _____

— My love _____ is wan-d'ring in star - flight. _____

BORN TO BE WILD

Words and Music by
MARS BONFIRE

MCA Music Publishing

nev - er want to die._____ Born to be wild.__

Born to be wild.__

Repeat and Fade

Born to be wild._____

COME SATURDAY MORNING
(Saturday Morning)
from the Paramount Picture THE STERILE CUCKOO

Words by DORY PREVIN
Music by FRED KARLIN

Come Saturday morning I'm
Come Saturday morning I'm

going away with my friend; We'll
going away with my friend; We'll

HANDS OF TIME
Theme from the Screen Gems Television Production BRIAN'S SONG

Words by ALAN BERGMAN and MARILYN BERGMAN
Music by MICHEL LEGRAND

DO YOU KNOW WHERE YOU'RE GOING TO?
Theme from MAHOGANY

Words by GERRY GOFFIN
Music by MIKE MASSER

FOR ALL WE KNOW

from the Motion Picture LOVERS AND OTHER STRANGERS

Words by ROBB WILSON and JAMES GRIFFIN
Music by FRED KARLIN

Moderato, with a light beat

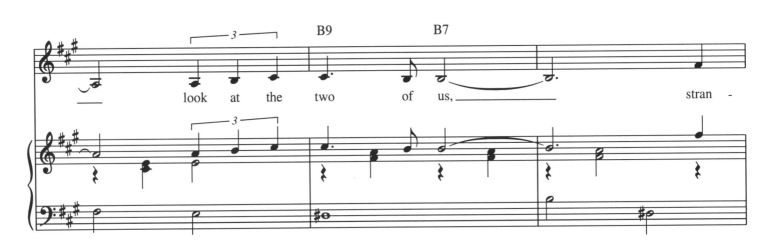

grow   for   all ___ we   know.

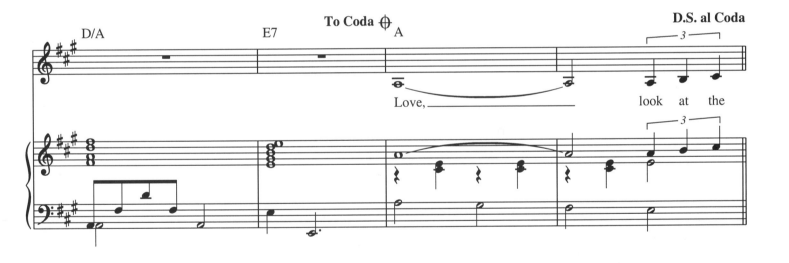

Love, _____ look   at   the

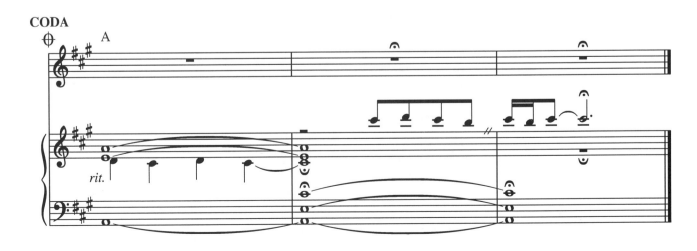

A Hard Day's Night

Words and Music by JOHN LENNON
and PAUL McCARTNEY

MOON RIVER

from the Paramount Picture BREAKFAST AT TIFFANY'S

Words by JOHNNY MERCER
Music by HENRY MANCINI

LOVE STORY
Theme from the Paramount Picture LOVE STORY

Music by FRANCIS LAI

NIGHT FEVER
from SATURDAY NIGHT FEVER

Words and Music by BARRY GIBB,
MAURICE GIBB and ROBIN GIBB

ONE TIN SOLDIER
from BILLY JACK

Words and Music by DENNIS LAMBERT
and BRIAN POTTER

Moderately slow rock tempo

Lis - ten child - ren to a sto - ry that was writ - ten long a - go__
So the peo - ple of the val - ley sent a mes - sage up the hill__
Now the val - ley cried with an - ger mount your hors - es, draw your sword__

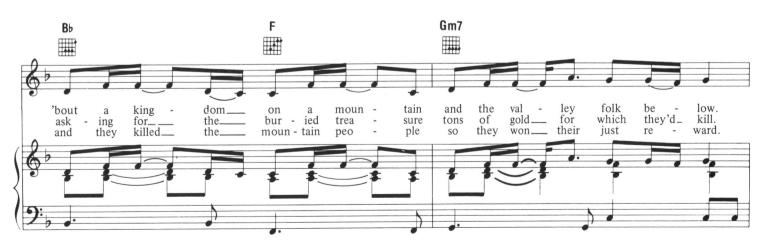

'bout a king - dom__ on a moun - tain and the val - ley folk be - low.
ask - ing for__ the__ bur - ied trea - sure tons of gold__ for which they'd__ kill.
and they killed__ the__ moun - tain peo - ple so they won__ their just re - ward.

RAINDROPS KEEP FALLIN' ON MY HEAD

from BUTCH CASSIDY AND THE SUNDANCE KID

Lyric by HAL DAVID
Music by BURT BACHARACH

ROMEO AND JULIET
(Love Theme)
from the Paramount Picture ROMEO AND JULIET

By NINO ROTA

TO SIR, WITH LOVE
from TO SIR, WITH LOVE

Words by DON BLACK
Music by MARC LONDON

Those   school   girl   days
The   time   has   come
Those   awk - ward   years

of   tell - ing   tales   and   bit - ing   nails   are   gone, _____
for   clos - ing   books,   and   long   last   looks   must   end. _____
have   hur - ried   by.   Why   did   last   they   fly   a - way? _____

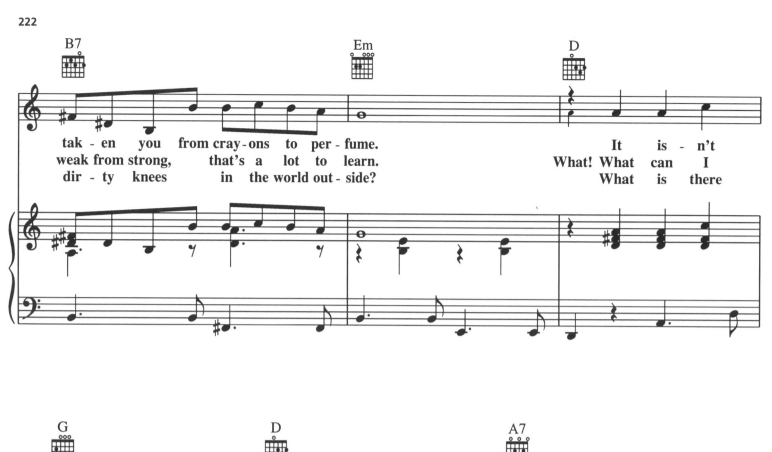

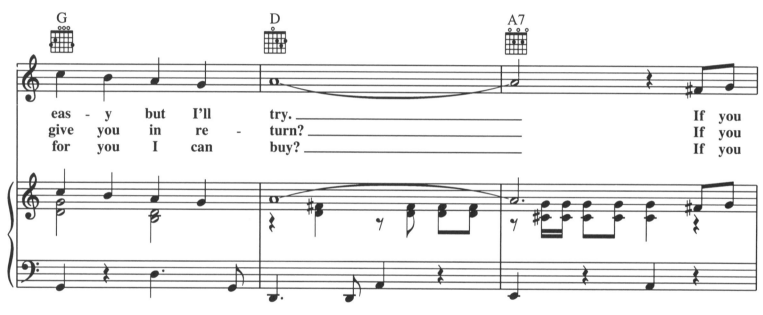

VIVA LAS VEGAS
from VIVA LAS VEGAS

Words and Music by DOC POMUS
and MORT SHUMAN

Very Brightly

THE WAY WE WERE

Words by ALAN and MARILYN BERGMAN
Music by MARVIN HAMLISCH

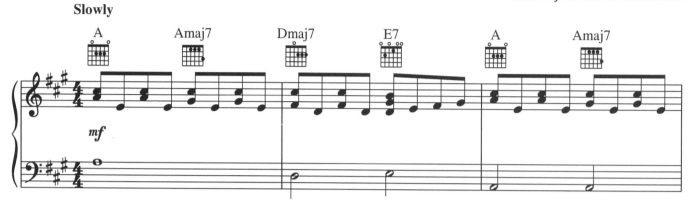

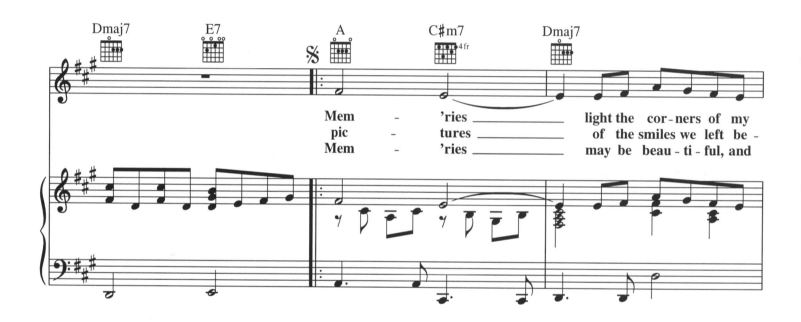

Mem - 'ries _____ light the cor-ners of my
pic - tures _____ of the smiles we left be -
Mem - 'ries _____ may be beau-ti-ful, and

mind.
hind, Mist-y wa-ter-col-or mem - 'ries _____
yet, smiles we gave to one an-oth - er _____
     what's too pain-ful to re-mem - ber _____

I'M POPEYE THE SAILOR MAN

Theme from the Paramount Cartoon POPEYE THE SAILOR

Words and Music by
SAMMY LERNER

MICKEY MOUSE MARCH
from Walt Disney's THE MICKEY MOUSE CLUB

Words and Music by
JIMMIE DODD

Mick - ey Mouse Club! Mick - ey Mouse Club! Who's the lead - er
Hey, there! Hi, there!

of the club that's made for you and me!
Ho, there! You're as wel - come as can be! M - I - C -

K - E - Y M - O - U - S - E! E! Mick - ey

ROCKY & BULLWINKLE
from the Cartoon Television Series

By FRANK COMSTOCK

THE SIAMESE CAT SONG
from Walt Disney's LADY AND THE TRAMP

Words and Music by PEGGY LEE
and SONNY BURKE

SUPERCALIFRAGILISTICEXPIALIDOCIOUS

from Walt Disney's MARY POPPINS

Words and Music by RICHARD M. SHERMAN
and ROBERT B. SHERMAN

MARY POPPINS
Sup-er-cal-i-frag-il-is-tic-ex-pi-al-i-do-cious!

E-ven though the sound of it is some-thing quite a-tro-cious,

If you say it loud e-nough, you'll al-ways sound pre-co-cious.

Winnie the Pooh

from Walt Disney's THE MANY ADVENTURES OF WINNIE THE POOH

Words and Music by RICHARD M. SHERMAN
and ROBERT B. SHERMAN